To My Husband, the man who taught me patience and reminds me often not to get in the ring with everyone. I Love You.

To My Children, I may not have always gotten it right, but I wasn't always wrong either. Thank you for loving me despite my flaws.

To My Girls Carla, Charlene, Gigi, and Quiana; Thank you for every conversation, for every piece of advice and for being rock stars.

TABLE OF CONTENTS

INTRODUCTION — 6

CHAPTER 1 — 9
TYPES OF CONFLICT — 9
Interpersonal — 9
Intrapersonal — 10
Intragroup — 11
Intergroup — 12

RESPONDING TO CONFLICT — **13**
Dealing with Intrapersonal Conflict — 16
Active Listening Skills — 21

RELATIONSHIP BOUNDARIES — 22
Social Norms — 29

CHAPTER 2 — **33**
COMMUNICATION STYLES — 33
Assertive — 33
Aggressive — 35
Passive Aggressive — 37
Submissive — 39
Manipulative — 41

NON-VERBAL COMMUNICATION — 46
Emotional Awareness — 49

IPY Agency LLC
1000 Parkwood Circle SE.
Suite 900
Atlanta, GA 30339

Copyright © 2018 Adrienne Alexander-Allen

All rights reserved. No part of this book may be reproduced in any form or by any electronic or mechanical means, including information storage and retrieval systems, without permission in writing from the publisher, except by reviewers, who may quote brief passages in a review.

ISBN-13: 978-0692164402
ISBN-10: 0692164405

Adrienne Alexander-Allen
Creating a Middle: Conflict Tips for the Modern World

Cover Design: Pro_Designx
Editor: Carla Dupont

Printed in the United States of America

www.theipyagency.com

****

Creating a Middle: Conflict Tips for the Modern World

Adrienne Alexander-Allen

CHAPTER 3 — **52**
RECOGNIZING CONFLICT — 52
Workplace Conflict — 54
Dominating Personalities — 58
Relationship Conflict — 67
Parent/Child Conflict — 75
I-Statements — 80

CHAPTER 4 — **88**
CONFLICT MANAGEMENT STRATEGIES — 88
Triggers — 97
Hot Button Topics — 107
Five Steps to Conflict Resolution — 110
Self-Awareness — 114

CHAPTER 5 — **123**
THE MIDDLE — 123
Conflict Resolution Skills — 125
Using What You've Learned — 131

Introduction

My journey to conflict management and conflict resolution has been an amazing and enlightening one. In the words of the late, great Langston Hughes, "Life for me ain't been no crystal stair. It's had tacks in it, and splinters and boards torn up."

Having parents who struggled with addiction, being a single mother, and moving to a new state without a support system, all forced me to focus and make things happen.

During my journey, the books I've read on conflict and the papers that I've researched, have mostly been in textbook form, not written with younger generations in mind.

Seeing the lack of youth focus or vibrancy in these books, along with the lack of tips dealing with conflict in urban communities, it became my mission to create a comprehensive, cohesive, and upbeat guide to conflict resolution that can be quickly read and understood in layman's terms for the masses.

So, what is conflict? Conflict is an opportunity for growth that can also be an effective means of creating dialogue among groups and individuals.

As a noun, the Latin word conflict means, "a serious disagreement or argument, typically a protracted one." As a verb, it means to be, "incompatible or at variance; clash." No matter the textbook definition of the word 'conflict,' the instant feeling of negativity one feels when hearing the word remains the same.

When we hear or see that someone is in conflict, we instantly think drama is coming next; but no more! This book will give you the skills and tools necessary to identify the type (s) of conflict you are dealing with, the steps required to effectively communicate your feelings and the ability to recognize conflict before it starts. Welcome to *Creating a Middle: Conflict Tips for the Modern World.*

As we begin our journey of learning how to deal with handling conflict effectively, it's a great idea to understand how we got to this point in the first place. Knowing that conflict is around us always, there are a couple of questions we should ask:

- When is it a good idea to take the next step in learning and trying to lessen the appearance of conflict?

- When do we begin to accept responsibility for our actions and take back the power that drama and negativity can have over us?

Did you know, an article in Forbes states that 90% of leaders lack people management skills and wish that they received proper training in resolving conflict?

Wow, so how does that translate to the employees working under them? Not only the employees, but these are also the same people we are entering relationships with and holding casual conversations with at the water cooler.

This book is here to help. Your voyage begins today. Along the way, you will learn how not to be a part of the 90% because you have become the ruler over your emotions and controller of your actions versus haphazardly reacting.

You, my friend, will become the king or queen of your castle. Well, maybe not so much that last part but you get where I'm going with this.

Let's start with the basics, discovering the different types of conflict, how they begin and what to look for when identifying the exact nature of the conflict you're dealing with.

CHAPTER ONE

Types of Conflict

Interpersonal conflict refers to a dispute between two individuals. This type of conflict typically occurs because of how people differ from one another. We have varied personalities which usually result in incompatible choices and opinions.

Examples:
- When your best-friend introduces you to their new friend
- Listening to someone in the mall having a full-blown conversation on speakerphone
- Tolerating your girlfriend who keeps taking back the guy who's cheating on her
- Dealing with the inconsiderate driver who cut you off.

Interpersonal conflict is a natural occurrence which can eventually help in personal growth and aid in developing your relationships with others.

Besides, making life adjustments is a necessary step in managing this type of conflict. However, when interpersonal conflict gets too destructive, calling in a mediator would help to have it resolved.

Intrapersonal conflict occurs within an individual; it's the internal dialogue we have when we walk into a room deciding who belongs and who doesn't.

It is the thought process that makes us think someone doesn't like us even though we've never had any personal interaction with the other person.

Because the experience takes place in the mind, intrapersonal conflict is psychological, involving individual thoughts, values, principles, and emotions.

Intrapersonal conflict manifests itself in many ways:
- Making simple decisions about hanging out with friends
- Making difficult choices regarding life paths and career goals

This type of conflict can be quite tricky to handle if you aren't in tune with your internal struggles.

Effects of dealing with *interpersonal* conflict may lead to restlessness and uneasiness, or in some cases, cause bouts with depression.

In extreme cases such as those mentioned, it could be a good idea to find a way to let go of the anxiety by talking it out with other people.

Finding ways to deal with intrapersonal conflict helps you to become more empowered as a person, thus evoking a positive change which will help you in your personal growth.

Intragroup conflict is a type of conflict that happens among individuals within a team. The incompatibilities and misunderstandings among these individuals lead to an intragroup conflict.

Intragroup conflict arises from interpersonal disagreements (e.g., team members have different personalities which may lead to tension) or differences in views and ideas (e.g., in a presentation, members of the team might find the notions presented by the one presiding to be erroneous due to their differences in opinion).

With most employees, intragroup conflict happens when one employee isn't handling the workload the same as the others, or when that one employee everyone knows never does any work complains they need more money.

When conflict arises in a team, it's a good idea to use that conflict as a teaching moment to help individuals reach their objectives together.

However, if the degree of conflict disrupts harmony among members, serious guidance from a knowledgeable party will help to achieve a swift, lasting resolution.

Intergroup conflict takes place when there's a misunderstanding between different teams within a company.

For instance, the marketing department of a company can come into conflict with the customer support department because of the diverse sets of goals and interests of these different groups.

The competition between groups also contributes to a rise in *intergroup* conflict. There are also other factors that fuel this type of conflict in urban settings such as:

- Micromanagement
- Superiority complexes that come with specific titles

Some of these factors may create a rivalry within resources or the creation of boundaries by a group to establish their own identity as a team.

Conflict may seem to be a problem to some, but this isn't how it should always be perceived.

Conflict is an opportunity for growth and can be an effective means of allowing yourself to speak freely amongst groups or individuals.

However, when the disagreement begins to prohibit productivity and gives way to more conflicts, proper conflict resolution skills are needed to find a resolution.

Responding to Conflict

There may be times when conflict teeters on the edge of destructiveness despite every effort being made to maintain a positive environment and promote constructive conflict.

You may bear witness to conflict, have someone bring a grievance to your attention, or a third party may make you aware of an ongoing dispute between others.

In either case, disputes and conflicts should always be acknowledged and a documented record made of the problem.

It is up to you to decide whether to intervene in a disagreement and if so, when is the right time.

Choosing to act in conflict will depend on many factors including how severe the conflict is, how many people are involved, and if this dispute will resolve on its own.

Minor conflicts will sometimes sort themselves out or can be solved with a little outside perspective. Harsher conflict situations will need to be addressed accordingly.

This would be a great time to ask yourself if this conflict is affecting your work. Are other employees and productivity being affected?

If you answer yes to either of these questions, the decision to intervene is no longer a choice, but a requirement.

Having decided to intervene in a conflict, you need to have clear guidelines on how you will help the feuding parties move forward towards a solution.

There are several different ways to intervene and respond to conflict, let's look at five specific approaches used universally to help you on your journey to becoming an expert.

Collaboration, also known as a win-win. Both parties work together to create a collaborative solution.

The needs of both groups are treated with equal importance. This approach helps build commitment and reduce bad feelings, but it can take some time.

Compromise, or win some-lose some. Both parties make some concessions to avoid damaging power struggles or to reach a solution quickly. This approach can become manipulative and create a cynical climate.

Competition, I win-you lose. One party uses force or coercion to resolve the conflict. This approach is aggressive and inflexible and can result in escalating conflict or retaliation.

Accommodation, lose-win. One party consents as a gesture of goodwill and lets the other party have their way. This approach can be used if the personal relationship is more important than the issue at hand. The downside to accommodation is that the yielding party can lose credibility.

Avoidance, lose-lose. Either party avoids the issue. This strategy is used if the problem is of low importance or if either party fears the risk of damage to the relationship or themselves. Feelings of frustration and resentment can often result from this approach.

When looking at the possible approaches, it is best to take each option and decide which to use based on the circumstances you know.

Which method will be the best strategic tactic?
Which will provide the best long-term solution?

Approaching conflict from this angle allows you to manage the long-term effects and will build credibility over time.

What's most important is to set the stage for taking your desired approach at the right time under the best conditions.

Dealing with Intrapersonal Conflict

When two parts of your brain are fighting against one another, this is an example of intrapersonal conflict.

Have you ever laid awake arguing with yourself because your mind was all over the place? Have you been overwhelmed with stress, guilt, or other emotions?

Intrapersonal or internal conflict happens when one part of you isn't in agreement with what the other part is doing.

These feelings typically manifest themselves in such high levels of discomfort that you believe something is going on that requires attention.

So, what are some signs of an internal conflict?

- Restlessness
- Overthinking
- The inability to decompress/relax
- Unable to fall asleep

Because internal conflict usually causes an overwhelming amount of emotions, it's essential that you learn how to deal with and subsequently end these conflicts.

I'm going to list out a few tips for you to help combat internal conflicts:

1. Don't ignore or suppress worrisome thoughts:

If you have an internal conflict, you will become frustrated, annoyed and irritated; especially, if your mind is wandering during a time that you are trying to sleep or relax.

Ignoring or suppressing these thoughts will only make them more intense. The best response is to let your subconscious mind know you received the message so that it will stop repeatedly replaying to get your attention.

Think of the possibilities, the options you have, and possible ways to get out of this mood instead of pushing those thoughts to the side.

2. Don't violate your values:

A principal source of internal conflict is the violation of your beliefs.

When you do opposite of what you believe in, it is your subconscious mind's job to get you back on track, and this causes your brain to start fighting itself.

Do your best to stick to your beliefs and if it so happens that you violate any of your values, make sure you don't allow it to happen again.

Internal conflict is usually triggered when there is a constant violation of values instead of when small deviations occur.

3. Keep Your Word:

The other primary source of internal conflict is not doing what you were supposed to do.

Your beliefs, goals, and values will always dictate that you act a certain way.

Not keeping up with the expectations you place on yourself or procrastinating will always result in severe internal conflict.

4. Write it down:

I've found that one of the best ways to deal with the unwanted noise in my brain is to write the thoughts down.

Writing down your feelings helps you feel as if you've been able to offload overwhelming emotions.

In addition to the sense of taking some of the weight off your shoulders, you also get self-understanding that will help you determine the best method to use to resolve that conflict.

5. Pay attention to your timeline:

As we reach different milestones in life, it sometimes seems that we use our peers as a litmus test for where we should be in life.

Being prepared for each stage and having a plan will decrease the likelihood of seeing what appears to be someone doing better than you or reaching a milestone before you.

However, if you haven't prepared yourself, seeing the success of others will undoubtedly bring about internal conflict.

As with most things, there will be times when you must take serious action to resolve internal conflict.

If, for example, you are uncomfortable taking orders, then indeed working for someone will harbor an internal conflict because part of you knows you need the job while the other part of you wants to work for yourself.

Personally, wanting to work for myself but needing to have consistent income has always been the case for me.

I was feeling underwhelmed and suffering through the desires of my heart for the realities of my pockets, so I decided to start my own business in parallel to my office job.

After a few months, I began to feel more relaxed. This parallel reassured me that there was a way out and working for someone else was not the end.

In other words, taking serious action and creating a plan can resolve most internal conflicts even if the main problem hasn't been fixed.

Active Listening Skills in Conflict

We should apply active listening skills when dealing with conflict, as well as making sure we know how to recognize the conflict, so we know when to intervene.

Examples of active listening include

- Building trust and establishing rapport.
- Demonstrating concern.
- Paraphrasing to show understanding.
- Nonverbal cues which show understanding such as nodding, eye contact, and leaning forward.
- Brief verbal affirmations like "I see," "I know," "Sure," "Thank you," or "I understand."
- Asking open-ended questions.

- Asking specific questions to seek clarification.
- Waiting to disclose your opinion.
- Communicating similar experiences to show understanding.

Boundaries in Conflict

In your adult life, I'm almost positive that you've either been told that someone crossed the line and needed to have boundaries set or you may have crossed a boundary line and had to address your actions to reel yourself back in.

With those things being said, what exactly are boundaries and how do we know when we've crossed the line?

Like boundary lines that separate neighborhoods and properties, boundaries exist in relationships.

These boundaries are emotional and physical spaces between yourself and someone else, or between you and several individuals at once.

When I think of boundaries, I always imagine someone being in my personal space, they have stepped over the imaginary line that has been drawn to ensure that I am comfortable in any given situation.

Walking into someone's personal space is not the only type of boundary that can be crossed.

Let's discuss some boundary types now.

New Friendships

Social media has made us so disconnected that creating new friendships has become a quiet place many chose not to visit.

DJ Khaled solicited a few high-power celebrities including Drake, Lil Wayne, and Rick Ross to make a song called "No New Friends." If that doesn't speak to the tension surrounding making new friends, nothing else will.

The stress we feel is because the friends you have, are accustomed to you, they know your behaviors, and you know theirs.

When it comes to making new friends, you must decide if this person is worthy of the time commitment involved in building an excellent foundation for that relationship.

Intimate Relationship

There's always a lot of chatter that goes on surrounding what should or shouldn't happen regarding boundaries in a relationship.

We expect our significant other to be fully aware of what we need, what we like, what we don't like, and so on.

It's very similar to debating whether you should or shouldn't ask your fiancé to sign a prenuptial agreement, you know you love them and want to be with them, but you also want to protect your assets. This is where boundaries help.

Relationships can't reach their full potential until both partners communicate their boundaries clearly and mutually respect one another.

Healthy relationships have boundaries whether they were predetermined in conversation or if they are discovered on the backend.

Below is a list of healthy and unhealthy aspects in a relationship: (from break the cycle.org)

Healthy	Unhealthy
Feeling responsible for your happiness	Feeling incomplete without your partner

Friendships exist outside of the relationship	Relying on your partner for happiness
Open and honest communication	Game-playing or manipulation
Respecting differences in your partner	Jealousy
Being honest about your wants	Feeling unable to express what is wanted
Accepting endings	Unable to let go

Here are a few tips to help you get started establishing boundaries with your partner in your relationship.

- Communicate your thoughts with one another. Be honest, but respectful when sharing your thoughts and feelings with your partner. It's healthy and okay to need time to gather your thoughts and feelings, but don't use that approach to avoid the conversation.

- Never assume or guess your partner's feelings. Making assumptions can create misunderstandings in a relationship.

You may feel you know your partner well enough to understand what they want or need without asking them, but it is always better to ask than to assume.

- Follow through on what you say. Setting boundaries and not executing them lets the other person think they have an excuse to continue to overstep your boundaries. You shouldn't make any exceptions to your boundaries without careful consideration because you may soon find yourself compromising on things that aren't acceptable to you.

- Take responsibility for your actions. Instead of immediately blaming your partner for the situation or how you're feeling, take a step back and think about the choices you've made in the relationship to see if they may have contributed to the situation. Both partners should be doing this!

- Know when it's time to move on. You can only share how you desire to be treated in the relationship, and you can't be responsible for your partner's feelings or communication.

Everyone has the right to be treated with respect and fairness. If your partner can't respect your boundaries, then it may be time to reevaluate the relationship.

Workplace Relationship

Working with someone for eight hours a day, five days a week can create a feeling of closeness that can make coworkers feel like family.

You share intimate conversations, watch each other's children grow up and even socialize outside of work hours.

Coworkers may be the ones closest to you when you are going through personal things in your life, and although you have a great rapport with them, boundaries should be set to protect your privacy.

As a manager, there is a need to balance closeness with your team through openness, yet a sense of objectivity and distance is required to make business decisions effectively.

Below are different types of boundaries and their characteristics:

- Personal: Values, Needs, Feelings, Thoughts

- Organizational: Values, Culture(s), Roles, Expectations
- Legal: Laws, Regulations, Court decisions
- Community: Values, Cultures, Expectations

Boundaries are normal and healthy; but, without proper communication surrounding boundaries, they can lead to uneasiness or embarrassment.

When we aren't aware that a boundary exists, we may be caught off guard or uncomfortable when that boundary is expressed by someone else.

There may have been tension after a joke you made in the workplace was deemed inappropriate by others, or you felt uncomfortable because of the actions of someone else; whether you reacted or not, a boundary needed to be expressed.

Not expressing your feelings regarding the boundary line that was crossed can create unnecessary tension and discomfort not only for yourself but also for others around you.

Being able to express and assert authority over your boundaries can be empowering and help guide the path to effective communication in your relationships.

Always remember, any negative feelings you may have regarding expressing your boundaries to others or others expressing boundaries to you, is temporary.

The anxiety that may present itself during tough conversations is a benefit and an indicator that you want the best outcomes yet may be unsure of how those outcomes may be perceived by the other party.

Setting boundaries can help us feel a sense of predictability and freedom. It can increase our self-esteem and confidence. We can feel happier and safer in our relationships with others.

We learn to develop ourselves personally and professionally through learning to respect our boundaries and the boundaries of others.

We can prevent unnecessary conflict that might lead to uncomfortable tensions as well as manage conflict by setting boundaries.

Social Norms

As we discuss boundaries, we must also consider social norms which often tend to challenge boundaries without warning.

From a sociological perspective, social norms are "informal understandings that govern the behavior of members of a society."

That means these behaviors are not rules per se, but more of a routine occurrence that has become recognized by society as a way of life.

Social psychology recognizes smaller group units, such as a team or an office, may also endorse norms separately or in addition to cultural or societal expectations.

In other words, norms are regarded as collective representations of acceptable group conduct, as well as individual perceptions of a groups conduct.

They can be viewed as cultural products (including values, customs, and traditions) which represent individuals' basic knowledge of what others do and think that they should do.

A perfect example of social norms in the classroom or anywhere that individuals frequent on a routine basis, is the response to unassigned seating.

Have you noticed that people tend to sit in the same seat every time they attend class or church? Or maybe you have your favorite spot in the breakroom to eat lunch, favorite stall in the public restroom or during your commute, you sit in the same area of the bus.

These are all examples of social norms and territorial behavior surrounding seat assignments.

By nature, when we choose a seat, we are adopting a place that makes us comfortable for a variety of reasons.

Maybe you like to sit close so that you can hear the teacher or minister better; perhaps you want to sit alone and in your personal space, or you want to be close to a friend.

Whatever the reason, once that seat has been chosen the first time, there is a routine to mentally assign that seat as your own although there is no rule saying that seat assignments must be made.

Quiet as it is kept, sitting in the same chair not only benefits you, but it becomes a guideline for people around you.

Individuals around you are now able to use you as a litmus test for where their seat is, as well as being able to recognize when you are absent.

Professors can use the unwritten seat assignments as well, so beware of the downside of sitting in the same place every day.

Most professors will look for you in your self-assigned seat; when you aren't there, it becomes noticeable that the seating arrangement has changed.

Sitting in the same seat every day helps to form bonds and build relationships while also avoiding tensions that may arise when trying to 'renegotiate' seat assignments.

Being creatures of habit, we, as human beings, have an innate need to be as comfortable as much as possible. Following a routine helps tremendously with that.

●●●

CHAPTER TWO

Communication Styles

Learning to identify communication styles and recognizing which ones we use in our daily exchanges with friends, family, and colleagues, is essential if we want to develop useful, confident communication skills.

This chapter will discuss various communication styles and how to differentiate between those styles.

For so long, only four communication styles were discussed, and those styles were Assertive, Aggressive, Passive-Aggressive and Submissive. Later, we would add another communication style, Manipulative.

Each of these styles has characteristics, language, and behaviors that are unique only to them, so let's learn about communication styles.

The Assertive Style

Assertive communication is typically found in individuals with a high level of high self-esteem.

Being assertive is arguably the healthiest and most effective style of communication as this is the middle of the road between being too aggressive and too passive.

When we assert ourselves, we have the confidence and ability to communicate without resorting to games or manipulation.

As an assertive communicator, you know the message you are sending, and you don't allow yourself to be swayed just because someone needs something from you or because of how the masses see things.

For as many people who seem confident and have high self-esteem, assertive communication tends to be the communication style that is used the least out of the five.

Non-Verbal Behavior
- Achieve goals without hurting others.
- Be protective of your rights, yet respectful of others' rights.
- Socially and emotionally expressive.
- Make choices and take responsibility for them.
- Ask directly for needs to be met, while open to the possibility of rejection.
- Accept compliments.

- Voice – medium in speed and volume.
- Posture – open posture, symmetrical balance, tall, relaxed, no fidgeting.
- Gestures – even, rounded, expansive
- Facial expression – good eye contact.
- Spatial position – in control, respectful of others.

The Language of Assertive Communication

- "Please, would you turn the volume down? I'm struggling to concentrate."
- "I am so sorry, but I won't be able to help you with your project today; I have an appointment."

Assertive communicators know where they stand with people and they're able to accept criticism and compliments. They can look after themselves and know how to show respect for the other person.

The Aggressive Style

Being aggressive while communicating is more about the win than it is about genuinely being communicative and usually comes at the expense of someone else's feelings.

An aggressive person expresses themselves as if their needs are the only needs worth considering and feel their feelings take precedence over anyone else who is trying to communicate.

The aggressive communication style is ineffective as the message may be missed due to the delivery and the tone in which it was received.

Non-Verbal Behavior

- Frightening, threatening, loud, hostile
- Willing to achieve goals at the expense of others
- Out to 'win.'
- Demanding, abrasive
- Belligerent
- Explosive, unpredictable
- Intimidating
- Voice – volume is loud.
- Posture – 'bigger' than others.
- Gestures - big, fast, sharp/jerky.
- Facial expression – scowl, frown, glare.
- Spatial position - Invade others' personal space, try to stand 'over' others.

The Language of Aggressive Communication

- "You get on my nerves!"

- "Do what I said!"
- "You make me sick!"

Sarcasm, name-calling, threatening, blaming, and insulting are a regular part of aggressive communicators' arguments.

Dealing with an aggressive communicator can create an environment that makes you feel angry, defensive, resentful, hurt, or afraid.

It is very common for individuals to lose respect for an aggressive person due to fear of being exploited or humiliated.

Problems are usually not reported to an aggressive person out of fear they may 'blow up.'

Passive-Aggressive Style

The style that completely grinds my gears and boils my blood is the Passive-Aggressive communication style.

With passive-aggressive communication, people appear passive on the surface but are hiding their anger indirectly. They are throwing stones, then hiding their hands, as my grandmother used to say.

This communication style usually comes from a place of feeling powerless and resentful, so these individuals express their feelings by subtly undermining the object of their resentments even if this ends in self-sabotage behavior.

Non-Verbal Behavior

- Sarcastic
- Devious
- Unreliable
- Winey
- Sulky
- Patronizing
- Gossips
- Smiles in your face and talks about you behind your back (rumors, sabotage, etc.)
- Voice – Often speaks with a sugary sweet voice.
- Posture – often asymmetrical, e.g., Standing with hand on hip, and hip thrust out (when being sarcastic or patronizing).
- Gestures – Can be jerky, quick.
- Facial expression – Often looks sweet and innocent.
- Spatial position – often too close, even touching others as they pretend to be warm and friendly.

The Language of Passive-Aggressive Communication

Passive-aggressive language tends to be attention seeking or a cry for attention. These communicators are usually filled with sarcasm or self-deprecation with a whiny type of feel.

A person using passive-aggressive communication may say something like, "Why don't you go ahead and do it? My ideas aren't fascinating anyway," or "Oh, don't worry about me. I can sort myself out – like I usually have to."

The Submissive Style

Submissive communication is mostly self-explanatory, this style is usually reserved for people pleasers and those who try to avoid conflict at all costs.

A submissive person behaves as if other peoples' needs are more critical and that other people have more rights and more to contribute.

Submissive communication is not to be confused with avoidance which is when someone wants to avoid conflict by not sharing their feelings for personal reasons.

Practicing avoidance in a conversation typically would fall under the label of the aggressive communication style.

Non-Verbal Behavior

- Overly apologetic.
- Avoids confrontation.
- Unable to accept responsibility or make decisions.
- Always giving in to others.
- Always the victim.
- Unable to receive compliments.
- Voice – Soft-spoken.
- Posture – Head down; tries to avoid being seen.
- Gestures – fidgety.
- Facial expression – no eye contact.

The Language of Submissive Communication

The following are examples of submissive communication statements typically used by submissive communicators.

- "Oh, it's nothing."
- "Oh, that's all right; I didn't want it anymore."
- "Whatever you choose is fine."

People on the receiving end of submissive communication feel:

- Exasperated
- Frustrated
- Guilty
- Taken advantage of

Others resent the low energy surrounding the submissive person and will give up trying to help them because their efforts are subtly or overtly rejected.

The Manipulative Style

To manipulate someone means to control or influence (a person or situation) cleverly, unfairly, or deceitfully, which is precisely how the manipulative communication style rolls.

This style is scheming, calculating, and shrewd. Manipulative communicators are skilled at influencing or controlling others to their advantage.

Their spoken words hide underlying messages, which are usually hidden from the other person. Have you ever heard the saying that someone could, "Sell water to a whale?" If so, that person was a manipulator.

Non-Verbal Behavior

- Cunning
- Insidiously controlling of others – for example, by sulking.
- Asking indirectly for needs to be met.
- Making others feel obliged or sorry for them.
- Uses 'artificial' tears.
- Voice – patronizing, envious, ingratiating, often high pitched.
- Facial expression – can put on the 'hang dog' expression.

The Language of Manipulative Communication

"You are so lucky to have those; I wish I had some. I can't afford things like this."

"I didn't have time to buy anything, so I wore this dress. I hope I don't look too awful in it." ('Fishing' for a compliment).

People receiving manipulative communication feel:
- Used
- Guilty
- Frustrated
- Angry, irritated or annoyed

- Resentful

The feeling of never knowing where you stand with a manipulative person makes individuals annoyed at continually having to work to find out what is going on with them.

●●●

Communication is an essential part of any healthy relationship with most of us needing to learn how to share and interact more effectively.

●●●

Please understand, communicating isn't just about words; communication includes tone of voice, facial expressions, body language, and even silence.

Unresolved conflict is like a Band-Aid, you can't place a Band-Aid over a wound without the proper care and expect the wound to heal correctly.

When you appropriately deal with conflict, it helps make your relationship stronger and more trusting.

One of the best ways to do this is to understand your way of communicating during a disagreement.

Not that we are promoting disagreements or arguments or even expecting them to happen, it's just that we all know they are bound to happen at some point.

Recognizing patterns will go a long way in helping to find a resolution.

The four main types of unhelpful communication patterns are:

- Attacking – attempting to control the outcome by use of force
- Defending – blocking another person's (perceived) attack
- Deflecting – directing attention away from you
- Freezing – feeling unable to respond because you are overwhelmed or frightened

The following activity is a great way to identify the pattern you use during a disagreement. Be sure to share this activity with your significant other so that both of you are on the same page with your respective communication styles.

Check the circles that relate to the way you disagree.

- Shouting (A)
- Acting as if it's nothing to do with you (B)
- Laugh it off (C)
- Become so upset you forget what you were arguing about (D)
- Name calling (A)
- Thinking about what you will say next while they are speaking (B)
- Not taking the issue seriously (C)
- Find your mind racing, unable to think clearly (D)
- Mocking or being sarcastic (A)
- Make excuses for your behavior (B)
- Change the subject (C)
- Unable to speak (D)
- Physically attack the other person (A)
- Refuse to talk about the issue (B)
- Find something else that is more important to do (C)
- Become physically immobile, weak or shaking (D)

Now that you've had an opportunity to read and learn about communication styles take a moment to reflect on your answers.

A = Attacking response, B = Defensive response, C= Deflective response and D= Freeze response

Do you use these behaviors when you communicate? What seems to be the primary way that you respond? Do you find yourself mainly in one group or several different groups? Was there a behavior missing from this list that you exhibit more often than others?

Once you've taken a moment to reflect and have looked over your answers, what could you do differently or how could you react differently in a disagreement?

Non-Verbal Communication

As women, we have a very distinctive use of non-verbal communication which I will neither confirm or deny is a good thing, you know? Girl code.

Our non-verbal cues are mostly displayed in the form of eye rolls, pursed lips, folded arms, tilting our head and the occasional lip pop.

In many instances, what comes out of our mouths (both men and women) and what we communicate through body language are two entirely different things, which leads to mixed signals.

When dealing with mixed signals, the individual on the receiving end of the conversation must decide whether the verbal or nonverbal message is most reliable.

As a heads up, most times, the person on the receiving end will choose the nonverbal message because it's a natural, unconscious language that broadcasts your true feelings and intentions.

According to The Importance of Effective Communication by Edward G. Wertheim, Ph.D., nonverbal communication cues can play five roles:

- Repetition: They can repeat the message the person is making verbally.
- Contradiction: They can contradict a message the individual is trying to convey.
- Substitution: They can substitute for a verbal message. For example, a person's eyes can often send a far more vivid message than words.
- Complementing: They may add to, or complement, a verbal message. A boss who pats a person on the back, in addition to giving praise, can increase the impact of the word.

- Accenting: They may accentuate or underline a verbal message. Pounding the table, for example, can highlight a message.

The important thing to understand about nonverbal communication is that it cannot be faked.

When preparing for a meeting or an interview, you may have been told to sit straight, don't slouch and offer a firm handshake so that you come across as confident and comfortable in your position.

However, most times these tricks won't work because inside, you're not confident or comfortable at all.

The reason for this is because we can't always control the signals we're sending out subconsciously. I'm sure you've heard the saying, "You don't have a poker face," or "You have a great poker face."

People who have mastered the poker face have better control of their nonverbal communication style than others.

They have trained themselves how to react, how to respond, and how to keep their feelings on the inside.

Most of us, however, are very reactionary, when we see something that stinks, we respond. You say something we don't like, we respond, and because the other person is standing in front of you receiving your nonverbal cues, they will react accordingly.

Being aware of your nonverbal cues will significantly aid you in your journey of communicating effectively and will help with the amount and accuracy of your nonverbal cues.

To do this, you need to be aware of your emotions and the effect they have on you. You should also be able to recognize the feelings of others and the message behind the cues they are sending. This is where we learn about emotional awareness.

●●●

Emotional Awareness

Emotional awareness enables you to:

- Accurately read other people, the emotions they're feeling, and the unspoken messages they're sending.
- Create trust in relationships by sending nonverbal signals that match up with your words.
- Respond in ways that show others you understand and care.
- Know if the relationship is meeting your emotional needs, giving you the option to either repair the relationship or move on.

As you work to develop your ability to recognize your own emotions, you'll become better equipped at understanding and identifying nonverbal cues.

Pay attention to contradictions between what you are seeing and what is being said. Look at nonverbal cues as a group as opposed to focusing on individual gestures or signals.

Consider all the cues you are receiving, from eye contact to tone of voice and body language. Overall, ask yourself if the nonverbal cues are consistent — or inconsistent — with what they are saying?

We must trust our instincts and what our gut is telling us. If you feel that someone isn't honest or that something isn't adding up, you may be picking up on a mismatch between verbal and nonverbal cues which could lead to arguments or disagreements.

Use the following guidelines when working to evaluate nonverbal signals.

- Eye contact – Is eye contact being made? If so, is it overly intense or, just right?
- Facial expression – What is their face showing? Is it masklike and unexpressive, or emotionally present and filled with interest?
- Tone of voice – Does the person's voice project warmth, confidence, and excitement, or is it strained and blocked?
- Posture and gesture – Is their body relaxed or stiff and immobile? Are shoulders tense and raised, or relaxed?
- Touch – Is there any physical contact? Is it appropriate for the situation? Does it make you feel uncomfortable?
- Intensity – Does the person seem flat, cold, and disinterested, or over-the-top and melodramatic?

- Timing and place – Is there a natural flow of information back and forth? Do nonverbal responses come too quickly or too slowly?
- Sounds – Do you hear sounds that indicate caring or concern?

CHAPTER THREE

Recognizing Conflict

Most times when we see conflict brewing, we become nervous because we see conflict as a sign that something has gone wrong or something is in the process of going wrong.

Think about critical indicators that alert you to conflict. You may notice people not getting along, loud voices or tension in a room gets thick.

In independent organizations, small doses of conflict are natural and necessary as this is a sign that the group is sharing in leadership and decision-making roles.

Being aware of this can help make conflict constructive rather than destructive.

We know from the introduction that conflict is a disagreement between at least two individuals who, because they assume they have different goals, may feel that the other party is preventing them from achieving those goals.

The great thing is that conflict doesn't always have to come from a place of varying opinions; conflict can arise even when people agree and have very similar goals.

When this happens, it is because information isn't being shared and the parties involved are acting on incomplete information which leads to making incorrect assumptions.

An omission of information, deliberately or not, can also create conflict.

Conflict can also occur when people negatively perceive the actions of the other party involved. They have become accustomed to judging one another negatively, so it has become a habit.

When we act in this manner, it makes everything that we say or do seem contrary even when that isn't the case; this then becomes more of a personal or internal conflict.

Individuals have different assumptions, values, and ideas, most of which are subconscious, so they hold onto these emotions and feelings without even realizing it.

These negative feelings will then cause individuals to make unconscious judgments about each other, and because these feelings are so deeply embedded into one's psyche, they become the most difficult to address.

This is because negative feelings and emotions need to be accepted and revealed which can be painful. Revealing unconsciously held emotions, biases, and judgments is a requirement for addressing conflict, which without being treated, may lead to no resolution at all.

Workplace Conflict

Typically, when a conflict in the workplace is happening, it begins with a bubble. Most workplace conflict is kept under wraps for a significant amount of time or until we've, "Had it up here," and are no longer able to remain professional.

Below are nine signs that indicate when a problem is beginning to bubble. Of course, these aren't the only signs; but, they are probably seen most often.

As a rule of thumb, anything that stunts the growth of productivity and positive interactions between employees and management is a sign that something is wrong and will need to be addressed before it gets out of hand.

- Dysfunctional meetings. Do staff meetings end up in a power struggle or verbal back-and-forth instead of employees being able to put their heads together to brainstorm? Is there a person or people you recognize as always trying to dominate the conversation or need to have the last word while others around appear annoyed or distracted?

- Anger. Any anger, but especially that which is an over-reaction, needs to be addressed immediately. Anger is rarely the response for a first-time upset.

- Productivity slowdowns. Are your employees daydreaming, calling out on a regular basis, or arriving late to work more often? When people are not happy with their work or the work environment, they tend to focus less. Pay attention to any declines in productivity and make attempts to pinpoint when things began to go downhill.

- High turn-over. If you notice a lot of come-and-go with your employees, unfortunately, there's a reason for that. No one enjoys the stress and frustration of looking for a job, so the fact that you can't retain staff is indicative of internal problems.

- Loss of trust. Trust is an essential part of any working relationship. Whether it be the trust between coworkers or between employees and leadership, instances of distrust within the company need to be addressed.

- Anxiety. Are there certain individuals who seem anxious or on edge most of the time? Maybe they avoid social interactions, always doubt their work or ask lots of questions. The presence of anxiety is often a sign that there may be underlying interpersonal issues brewing.

- Clique forming. The goal is for employees to be working together as a team, however, if you are seeing cliques form or the same employees teaming up on projects, the company isn't functioning and is not being as productive as possible.

- Repetitive disagreements. Does it seem that the same employees always disagree on petty things? If you hear of two people going back-and-forth in the breakroom do you already have an idea of who it is?

  Addressing these types of communication issues is essential to maintaining balance and stopping conflict before it gets out of control.

- Inappropriate communications. Rude emails or emails that use inappropriate language, rudeness in speech, or disregard for the opinion of others is an indicator that conflict is present and someone is on the verge of blowing up soon.

So, what can you do when you recognize workplace conflict? That's why Creating a Middle is here!

When you notice these or other situations indicating that trouble is brewing, do not assume the issue will resolve itself – all disruptions in the workplace need to be addressed as soon as possible, if not immediately by your team leader, HR staff, or yourself.

In many cases, a professional conflict specialist can help everyone get to the core cause of the conflict and help resolve any issues.

If you need help figuring out your next move, consult a professional who can give you the tools needed to determine the underlying conflict or pull out this book.

By being proactive about these early warning signs, you give your company a chance to continue growing and running efficiently along with the ability to manage conflicts that could cause a loss of employees and weaken productivity.

Dominating Personalities

Most work environments have at least one individual who tends always to dominate the team. Unfortunately, it can be found that a project isn't going well because that dominant team member continually shuts down everyone else's suggestions and opinions to focus on what they believe should happen.

In this situation, take a step back for a moment to establish the best course of action to resolve and redirect this person's behavior.

To do this, we need to ascertain why this person is behaving this way? We must identify those core issues, then decide what we need to do to get the team back working together collaboratively and pressing forward towards a more productive work environment.

In thinking of ways to resolve this conflict, the first step is to re-address appropriate behavior within a business meeting and to identify roles for key individuals within the meeting group.

While doing this, assign someone to take notes, a timekeeper, and someone who might play the mediator role to ensure there's a balance between everyone's rights to have their voice expressed during all meetings.

Use the following steps to shift focus away from the dominant person and their agenda as a guideline to getting the ball rolling back in the right direction.

Keep Cool and Maintain Your Composure

One of the most common characteristics of a controlling and dominating personality is their deliberate attempt to upset you, push your buttons and activate your triggers.

By doing this, they create an advantage over you, from which they can exploit your weakness.

The less reactive you are to be provoked, the more you can use your better judgment to handle the challenge.

When you feel upset with or challenged by someone, before you say or do something you might regret later, take a deep breath and count slowly to ten.

In many instances, by the time you reach ten, you would have regained composure, and figured out a better response to the issue. This helps to reduce, instead of exacerbating the problem.

If you're still upset after counting to ten, take a time out if possible, and revisit the issue after you calm down.

If necessary, use phrases such as "I'll get back to you…" or "Let me think about it…" to buy yourself some time. By maintaining self-control, you leverage more power to manage the situation.

Taken from https://www.psychologytoday.com

Keep Your Distance and Keep your Options Open

Not all aggressive or dominating individuals are worth your time. Your time is valuable, and your happiness and well-being are most important.

Unless there's something significant at stake, don't overwhelm yourself by trying to spar with a person who's negatively entrenched verbally.

Whether you're dealing with an angry driver, a pushy relative, or a domineering supervisor, keep a healthy distance, and avoid engagement unless you absolutely must.

There may be times when you may feel you're "stuck" with a complicated person, and there's "no way out." In these situations, consult with trusted friends and advisors about different courses of action, with your well-being as the number one priority.

Depersonalize and Shift from Reactive to Proactive

Being mindful of the nature of aggressive, intimidating, and controlling people can help us de-personalize the situation and turn from being reactive to proactive.

One effective way to de-personalize is to put yourself in the other person's shoes, even if for just a moment.

For example, consider the offender you're dealing with, and complete the sentence: "It must not be easy…"

- "My friend is so aggressive. It must not be easy to come from an environment where everyone was forced to compete…"
- "My manager is really overbearing. It must not be easy to have such high expectations placed on her performance by senior executives…"
- "My partner is so controlling. It must not be easy to have grown up in a family where he was told how to think and act in every way…"

The point is to remind yourself that people do what they do because of their personal issues. If we're being reasonable and considerate, difficult behaviors from others say a lot more about them than they do about us.

By reducing personalization, we can be less reactive and concentrate our energy on problem-solving.

Know Your Fundamental Human Rights

An essential element to keep in mind when you're dealing with a difficult person is to know your rights and recognize when they're being violated.

If you aren't harming others, you have the right to stand up for yourself and defend your rights. On the other hand, if you bring harm to others, you may forfeit these rights.

The following are some of our fundamental human rights:

- You have the right to be treated with respect.
- You have the right to express your feelings, opinions and wants.
- You have the right to set your priorities.
- You have the right to say "no" without feeling guilty.
- You have the right to have opinions different than others.

Of course, society is full of people who do not respect these rights. Aggressive and dominating individuals want to deprive you of your rights so they can control and take advantage of you.

Don't let that happen; you have the power and moral authority to declare that it is you, not the offender, who's in charge of your life.

Focus on these rights and allow them to keep your cause just and strong.

Put the Spotlight on Them & Reclaim Your Power

A familiar pattern with aggressive and dominating people is that they like to place attention on you to make you feel uncomfortable or inadequate.

Typically, they're quick to point out there's something not right with you or the way you do things. The focus is consistently on "what's wrong," instead of "how to solve the problem."

This type of communication is often intended to dominate and manipulate, rather than to take care of issues sincerely.

If you react by being on the defensive, you fall into the trap of being scrutinized, thereby giving the aggressor more power while she or he picks on you with impunity.

A simple and powerful way to change this dynamic is to put the spotlight back on the difficult person, and the easiest way to do so is to ask questions.

For example:

- Aggressor: "You're so stupid."
- Response: "If you treat me with disrespect I'm not going to talk with you anymore. Is this what you want?"

Keep your questions constructive and probing. By putting the problematic person in the spotlight, you can help neutralize her or his undue influence over you.

A second technique you can use to interrupt negative communication is to change the topic.

Merely say "By the way…" and initiate a new subject. When you do so, you're taking charge of the flow of communication, and setting a more constructive tone.

In Relatively Mild Situations, Display Superior Composure Through Appropriate Humor.

Humor is a powerful communication tool. Years ago, I knew a co-worker who was quite stuck-up and intimidating.

One day a colleague of mine said "Hello, how are you?" to him. When the egotistical co-worker ignored her greeting completely, my colleague didn't feel offended.

Instead, she smiled good-naturedly and quipped: "That good, huh?" This broke the ice, and the two of them started a friendly conversation. Brilliant.

When appropriately used, humor can shine a light on the truth, disarm challenging behavior, and show that you have excellent composure.

In Serious Situations, Set Consequences to Compel Cooperation

When an aggressive, intimidating, or controlling individual insists on violating your boundaries, and won't take "no" for an answer, deploy consequence.

The ability to identify and assert a consequence(s) is one of the most important skills you can use to "stand down" a complicated person.

Expertly articulated, consequence gives pause to the offending individual and compels her or him to shift from violation to respect.

Relationship Conflict

Relationships consist of two people with different perspectives, different values and of course, different personalities for the most part.

These people can subconsciously create conflict merely because they are not fully aware of or accepting of the differences in their relationship.

As we defined in the introduction, conflict typically refers to disagreements or different points of view between individuals.

However, dealing with conflict mostly comes down to individual behaviors and those individuals not knowing how to manage in certain situations.

Conflict is not a bad thing, assuming you are committed to the relationship and willing to find the kinks to work out. Don't be confused, conflict can be a blessing inside of a curse.

How is that, you ask? Simple, nothing is perfect. If you're in a relationship that has no bumps or conflict, someone's not being truthful.

Transparency is a necessity in a relationship. If the two of you always agree with what the other is saying, someone's holding back their real feelings, and actual points of view aren't being discussed.

Both parties in a relationship have the right to view things differently and to express those views without hurting the other's feelings.

When conflict arises, both partners are usually open and honest about their feelings while voicing their opinions to find common ground.

Conflict in relationships begins for many reasons, but before trying to fix conflict, you need to see what got you to that point in the first place.

Most times, the conflict remains because individuals focus on the surface of the problems; never digging deeper to find the cause.

Placing an invisible Band-Aid on the issue may ease the pain, end the argument, and make the symptoms go away temporarily but eventually, the problem(s) will continue.

Bubbling of conflict in personal relationships manifests itself by making everything the other person does a significant issue, i.e., why are you coughing so much? Why are you breathing so loud? Why didn't you compliment me today like you did the other day?

To keep things in perspective, remember that all relationships have disagreements. Conflict does not mean your partnership is a failure, nor does it say the two of you can't be happy.

Healthy relationships grow and mature through conflict. When individuals in relationships begin to become affected mentally or emotionally by conflict, speaking with a professional may help.

Brushing the issues under the rug, assuming you are mentally prepared and fully capable of solving significant problems on your own may become more of a hindrance than a help.

You and your partner can both benefit from the support of a therapist or relationship coach. Having someone who is neutral who can see the conflict from an outside perspective will create a path to healing that otherwise may have gone unnoticed.

As with workplace conflict, there are specific behaviors and causes to look for that lead to or create relationship conflict.

In small doses, these occurrences may seem minor or not an issue. Over time, however, not addressing small cracks in the foundation lead to significant problems that will prove to be costly. In this case, it may be your relationship that is lost.

I have outlined and explained five of the leading causes of conflict in relationships below. The five reasons outlined are not the only signs; just the most common.

But remember, same as with professional conflict, anything that stunts the growth of positive interactions between individuals in a relationship is a sign that something is wrong.

Those things must be addressed before they create significant changes to the foundation that can't easily be fixed.

Selfishness. In relationships, sometimes we are so focused on being *IN* a relationship that we forget our decisions affect others.

Honestly, this is true for all types of relationships. Couples often have a conflict because one person in the relationship isn't thinking of or considering the other person during the decision-making process.

When this is done knowingly and happens often, it extends the life of the conflict.

Selfishness will always be number one on the list of items that create conflict because a person who cannot respect the needs of others cannot also have healthy relationships, professional or personal.

Communication. How many times have you been told: "It's not what you say, but how you say it"? Voice, tone and overall communication is the method of sharing your thoughts and feelings with others.

Being unable to communicate effectively, creates conflict where there was none. Often, trying to talk to someone who chooses to keep their opinions to themselves, leads to an argument.

Trying to convince someone to communicate who doesn't want to, creates tension and as a result, communication channels are shut down and avoided.

Resentment. Being in relationships comes with a territory of ups and downs. The downs tend to include moments where things are said or done that can be deemed offensive by your significant other.

At that moment, if your significant other fails to apologize or explain the reason behind those things being said or done, it can cause resentment.

The same can be said if your significant other fails to communicate that they were hurt or offended and kept those feelings to themselves.

When individuals neglect to share how they are feeling, it creates a space of loneliness that can cause resentment.

Hiding feelings initiates the all too familiar, 'what's wrong' conversation where the answer is always, "Nothing." Yet, you see the distance, silence, and discontent that is shown by the other person.

It becomes frustrating to continue asking what's wrong knowing that the other party involved will brush it off.

It is crucial at this stage to try to find the cause of the conflict because without communicating the real issues, the other party may feel you are no longer interested in the relationship and begin to look for happiness elsewhere.

Finger Pointing or Criticism. It's always you and never them, right? People who criticize everything everyone else does without peeking in the mirror can be frustrating because they aren't able to accept responsibility for their actions.

In my opinion, the basis for finger pointing comes from a place of narcissism, but of course, that isn't always the case.

Often, individuals have not had an opportunity to share their feelings honestly or even been held to task for the things they have done wrong in the past.

A good idea for dealing with narcissistic or spoiled individuals who are never wrong is to seek outside help.

Someone who wants always to be right will typically keep this behavior until they are shown the error of their ways.

Unrealistic or Distorted Expectations. "Expectations breed disappointment," has been a saying to live by for me. If you ever take a step back to look at why you were hurt and disappointed with a situation, it was probably based on your expectations.

Expectations of how that individual should respond, what they should say, or how they should act. When situations don't play out the way they were 'supposed to,' was it based off what was communicated to you or based on the expectations you placed on the other person?

Life teaches us that we must be responsible for our happiness, placing unspoken expectations on the other person in our relationship, puts us in a position to be left with the hurt feelings.

It may be easier said than done, but don't place such emphasis on the other person and how they should respond. Learn to hear and receive what your significant other is saying versus listening to them speak so you can react.

Most times, people have already shared their capabilities with you; you just weren't in the right space to receive it.

Relationships have a conflict because one or both parties feel their side isn't being heard.

Being in a relationship, we tend to assume certain things should be unspoken and therein lies a trigger for conflict.

Being able to communicate your wants, needs, and desires effectively can help to alleviate occurrences of conflict although as previously stated, a little bit of conflict never hurt anybody.

Resolving Parent/Child & Child/Child Conflict

This subject is a doozy! Identifying communication styles in children is something that needs to start very early in life, along with establishing boundaries which we will discuss later.

Being able to resolve conflict is a social skill that children need from as early as the proverbial sandbox.

Parents differ on how to discipline their children from time-out to spankings to 'avoiding,' the latter being the worst decision parents can make.

The next set of steps will help you to resolve conflict with your children.

In return, these skills will help them as they grow older and need to deal with disputes greater than someone playing with their favorite toy or not agreeing with your curfew.

Calm Down

One thing I've learned, and a good rule of thumb is it's never a good idea to have an argument or disagreement in the heat of the moment. There is a significant amount of emotions at play, and things said out of anger, can't be taken back.

Take a moment to calm down while giving your child the same opportunity. Maybe walk away and blow off some steam in another room or count slowly from 1-100.

Sometimes sleeping it off is an option. All parties should be calm and in the right frame of mind before addressing conflict.

If your child is old enough, give them a pencil and some paper. Ask them to write down what they are feeling. Writing not only gives your child an opportunity to communicate without being interrupted, but it also gives you both a chance to clear your minds.

State & Understand the Problem

Once you've found yourself in a mentally and emotionally calm place, talk to your child or children and help them state their problem.

Explain to them the importance of open and honest communication while accepting their role in the conflict.

Accomplishing this task may be easier said than done because children (in their opinion) never do anything wrong.

The great thing, however, is that this process will help prepare them for the future.

Creating an environment where children are praised for their honesty, and the 'punishment fits the crime' usually goes over better when a child can see the part they played in the conflict that is happening.

Encourage the use of 'I' statements, so those involved aren't placed on the defensive due to their sharing.

Apologize Well

According to www.wikihow.com, "A good apology will communicate three things: regret, responsibility, and remedy.

Apologizing for a mistake might seem complicated, but it will help you repair and improve your relationships with others."

Apologies that tend to explain beyond the level of a typical apology, usually never fix the conflict. They are a way to skate over it.

Apologies that include the words 'but' and 'because' are also serve as a great way to keep the conflict going.

Help your child to understand the ingredients of a sincere apology. Including a handwritten apology with the initial writing while calming down is a great start.

The following are some excellent tips for creating an apology that works:

- Use the words, "I'm sorry."
- Acknowledge exactly how you messed up. (For example, "I used words that hurt your feelings.")
- Share with the person exactly how you plan to fix the conflict.

- Make a promise to behave better next time.
- Ask for forgiveness.

Bad apologies, on the other hand, tend to make matters worse because you aren't taking responsibility for your actions, i.e., justifying words or behavior; blaming the victim (I'm sorry but…); making excuses; and minimizing the consequences ("It was just a joke!").

Promote Solution Finding

Work with children to brainstorm solutions for their conflict. Because we've 'been there, done that,' it's effortless to feel like we have all the answers and that children should follow suit.

You will find that when children can come up with the solution themselves, they respect it more.

Encourage your child to listen to the other child if there's a conflict between friends, and to listen to you when in conflict with your child.

Highlight the importance of an open and honest conversation spoken in an even tone with kind words.

Speaking freely and openly creates an environment where children understand that they can share their feelings without being judged or fear of being reprimanded for sharing.

Follow-Up

Check in with your child regarding how they're feeling and find out if they're satisfied with their solution.

You always want to reinforce that coming to you to share their feelings isn't a mistake. Show genuine care and concern to make sure the problem has been resolved, and the appropriate solution has been reached as opposed to this being a temporary fix or Band-Aid over the issue.

'I' Statements

When dealing with conflict and learning to effectively communicate our feelings, it is essential to stick to expressing how you feel versus pointing fingers at the other person.

In interpersonal communication, use of an 'I' message or 'I' statement is a style of communication that focuses on your feelings or beliefs rather than projecting our thoughts and characteristics on the listener.

For example, you could tell your significant other, "I worry when you come home late consistently without updating me and letting me know you're safe," instead of demanding, "Why are you never home on time?"

The concept of 'I' statements was developed by Thomas Gordon in the 1960s while doing play therapy with children. He later added this concept to his book for parents, P.E.T.: Parent Effectiveness Training.

'I' statements are intended to be assertive without making blanket accusations or putting the listener on the defensive.

'I' statements are also used to take ownership of your feelings rather than implying that someone placed you in a contrary space.

For example, you could say: "I'm falling behind on my assignment because I don't have enough research rather than: "The reason we're behind is that you haven't finished your research in time!" (This is an example of a 'you-statement.')

When used correctly, 'I' statements promote positive communication in relationships and help them to become stronger.

By sharing feelings and thoughts honestly and openly, this can help partners grow closer on an emotional level.

'I' Statements in Therapy

My first experience with 'I' statements would be in a Communications Class at Morgan State University. When my professor began the lecture on conflict and the use of 'I' statements in a sharing assignment, I laughed because 'we' don't typically speak this way.

As a 30+-year-old woman, I'm thinking to myself, "Who wrote this?" However, after listening and further understanding the thought behind the use of 'I' statements, I understood it, and it made sense.

Most mental health professionals encourage people in therapy to use 'I' statements when communicating with others.

'I' statements are instrumental in couples counseling where blame is more prevalent than conversations that explore the cause of the negative emotions or underlying issues that lead to conflict in the beginning.

The use of 'I' statements allows individuals to work through their problems in a way that will enable them to freely express how they're feeling without placing blame and pointing fingers at their significant other.

Although 'I' statements are great conversation tools, there is still the opportunity for an 'I' statement to be misused.

For example, the speaker may say to their partner, "I hate it when you don't listen to me." This statement begins with an 'I,' but because of the tone of the comment, the potential is there for the meaning to be received as snappish and may not be the best way to express their feelings.

Better use of an 'I' statement could be, "I feel ignored and unloved when you don't listen to me." Specialists will help individuals practice appropriate 'I' statements and explore ways to respond to the feelings that these statements communicate.

'I' statements are often also used in family counseling because they focus on the child or the parent's actions rather than on the act itself.

Young adults and adolescents may be more receptive to hearing how their actions have affected others when the language used is not accusatory.

I understand that adults are not walking around making 'I' statements, the tone of 'I' statements can feel forced, coerced, or even silly, so it may take some practice to get into the rhythm of communicating correctly with 'I' statements.

To help you become more comfortable using 'I' statements, I have listed some examples below but will also include worksheets and exercises to help you along the way.

Examples of 'I' statements:

Your sister, sister-girl, mother, daughter, or auntie borrows your shirt and returns it with stains and a tear.

Typical response: "You ruined my shirt! I'm so sick of you! Are you ever going to grow up?!"

'I' statement response: "I'm angry because my shirt is messed up and I can't afford to replace it. I appreciate it when the things I loan you are taken care of and returned the same way they were when you borrowed them."

Your teenager is annoyed with you for continually asking if they've completed their homework.

Typical response: "Can you please stop asking me about my homework!"

'I' statement response: "It makes me feel frustrated and annoyed when I'm asked over and over about my homework. I am old enough to complete my homework without reminders."

Always remember, the sole focus of an 'I' statement is to express your feelings without making someone else feel upset.

'I' statements help to directly express feelings or opinions, without blaming, pointing fingers or accusing another person.

The purpose of 'I' statements is to help you take responsibility for how you feel and to help make the other person feel less defensive and more open to working with you to find a solution.

Listed are tips to help you on your journey to becoming more comfortable using 'I' statements.

- Avoid inserting words such as 'that' or 'like,' because they are often about an opinion or judgment.

- Don't use lines like 'I feel like you' or 'I feel that you.'
- Don't start with the word 'you,' because the 'you' sounds like blaming.
- Start by practicing expressing emotions like hurt, anxiety, or sadness before you show anger.
- It's generally harder to express anger through 'I' statements without it coming out as blame and attack.
- Remember to practice using positive 'I' statements, too.

Like anything, both parties often get better at this with practice. Just be aware, it is not about getting the anticipated response you want from the other person. The aim is to be respectful, regardless.

'I' Statements Worksheet & Role-plays

The following are examples of how to adequately convey an 'I' statement. To complete this worksheet, respond to the following situations with an 'I' statement.

I feel (state your feelings), when (state the undesired behavior you wish to stop), because (state why you feel the way you do) and (state your future expectations and or future consequences.

After mastering the formula, you may be more comfortable using a less structured statement.

Now, using the formula above, practice your 'I' statements using the following scenarios:

1.   Your spouse calls you from work to tell you he/she will be home in a half hour and he/she arrives home an hour and a half later. This is a weekly occurrence.

2.   Your friend calls the third time this month to cancel plans with you at the last minute to go out with their significant other.

3.   Your child tells you at 9:00 p.m., that she signed you up to bring cupcakes to school tomorrow for the class party and you have don't have the ingredients in the house.

4.   Your neighbor continually drops by expecting you to be able to watch her child at a moment's notice.

5. You are trying to leave the house by 8:00 to get to your job on time; however, your 3-year-old child is slow again this morning.

6. Your sister just borrowed your favorite sweater again without asking, and now it's dirty when you want to wear it.

CHAPTER FOUR

Conflict Management Strategies

When working towards effective conflict resolution, five strategies are typically used to make sure that cohesion is present in groups, personal and professional relationships.

Listed below are those five strategies along with an explanation of each so that they are easily recognizable to yourself and your teammates. *strategy content is taken from http://smallbusiness.chron.com/5-conflict-management-strategies-16131.html *

Accommodating

The accommodating approach essentially entails giving the opposing side what it wants. The use of accommodation often occurs when one of the parties wishes to keep the peace or perceives the issue as minor.

For example, a business that requires formal dress may institute a casual Friday policy as a low-stakes means of keeping the peace with the rank and file.

Employees who use accommodation as a primary conflict management strategy, however, may keep track and develop resentment.

Why being accommodating may not work

- Focuses on demands (vs. needs, perceptions, values, goals, feelings)
- Power is defined by what one side gets the other to concede
- Mini-version of conquest
- Spin-off conflicts emerge

Avoiding

The avoidance strategy seeks to put off conflict indefinitely. By delaying or ignoring the conflict, the avoider hopes the problem resolves itself without a confrontation.

Those who actively avoid conflict frequently have low esteem or hold a position of low power.

In some circumstances, avoiding can serve as a profitable conflict management strategy, such as when an unproductive employee is let go.

Hiring a more productive individual for the position will heal most of the conflict.

Why avoidance may not work

- Miss out on opportunities to learn and grow
- Merely postpones dealing with conflict
- Generally, it gets worse with time, not better
- Frustrations are unclarified
- Keeps people from learning about themselves and each other

Collaborating

Collaboration works by integrating ideas set out by multiple people. The object is to find a creative solution acceptable to everyone.

Collaboration, though useful, calls for a significant time commitment not appropriate to all conflicts.

For example, a business owner should work collaboratively with the manager to establish policies, but collaborative decision-making regarding office supplies wastes time better spent on other activities.

Why collaborating may not work

- Makes, "It's beyond my control," the mantra.
- Disempowers all sides; makes them slaves to bureaucracy.
- Limits options to what the 'rule book' says.
- Creates an adversarial role.

Compromising

The compromising strategy typically calls for both sides of a conflict to give up elements of their position to establish an acceptable, if not agreeable, solution.

This strategy prevails most often in conflicts where the parties hold approximately equivalent power.

Business owners frequently employ compromise during contract negotiations with other businesses when each party stands to lose something valuable, such as a customer or necessary service.

Why compromising may not work

- Gives the illusion that issues have been addressed.
- Things usually get worse.
- Devalues attempts at conflict resolution.
- Rewards the quicker fixer.
- Creates mistrust when things that 'got fixed' turn out to still be broken.
- Short circuits processes and abilities to address problems in the future.

Competing

Competition operates as a zero-sum game, in which one side wins and the other loses. Highly assertive personalities often fall back on competition as a conflict management strategy.

The competing approach works best in a limited number of conflicts, such as emergency situations.

In general, business owners benefit from holding the competitive strategy in reserve for crisis situations and decisions that generate ill-will, such as pay cuts or layoffs.

Why competing may not work

- Sets up a pattern of using power against each other
- Prevents the subordinate party to contribute to the relationship
- Reduces decisions to binary choices
- Creates desire for revenge
- 'Winner' must be on guard afterward

When dealing with these strategies, it is essential to create an environment that is conducive to receiving information that is being shared and a dialogue that is open to resolving conflict effectively.

Below are a few guidelines to follow to make sure you are on the right path to a solution.

Create an effective atmosphere:

- Choose someplace that is neutral to the conflict, so the parties involved don't feel threatened or backed into a corner.

- Avoid the bedroom! Intimate thoughts cloud judgment, and emotional connections may overshadow conflict resolution.
- Avoid distractions as much as possible. No background conversations, no busy windows, and outside noises.

Clarify perceptions

- Is this conflict with someone else or is it internal?
- What is the conflict about? What is it not about?
- What's your motivation and expected outcome? (opposing party)

What do I need? What am I expecting to happen?

- Focus on individual and shared needs
- Are there needs that aren't being met?
- Is my partner aware of my needs?
- If I don't receive the things I need, what will happen?
- What can be done to meet our individual needs?
- What happens if requirements aren't met within a specific timeframe?

Build positive shared power.

- Have a clear self-image
- Create consistency between values and behaviors
- Oversee yourself

Energize the power of your partner.

- Don't allow past negative behaviors define your partner.

Look to the future; learn from the past.

- Focus on the present and the future.
- Be willing to let go of old issues that are now irrelevant.
- Avoid the pigeonhole, "It's always been done this way."
- Remind each other of solid partnerships in the past.
- Encourage the process, focus on the power of forgiveness.

Generate options

- Brainstorm ideas that work
- Set aside previous ideas
- Look for commonalities

- Learn your partner's options, spend time learning about them
- Imagine yourself being your best self

Develop 'doables': stepping stones to action

- Relationships are made up of moments
- Build resolutions on stepping stones
- Meet shared needs
- Make sure doables are not just a Band-Aid or a quick fix

Make mutual-benefit agreements

- Replace demands; conflicts typically come from unrealistic demands
- Clarify responsibilities
- Keep the conflict resolution partnership alive
- Clarify perceptions as soon as conflict presents itself.

Working to combat conflict effectively is a group effort, but more importantly, it's a unique effort for you. As previously defined, conflict comes from a place of discord or friction that involves more than one person.

Having the skills and tools necessary to deal with conflict puts you at an advantage over those without proper training.

Conflict resolution skills also help put out fires before they grow out of control.

Remember, the strategies and guidelines I've given you are just that, guidelines and strategies. You have the power to make these tools your own and share them with your significant other, your coworkers, and even your children.

Triggers

We've had a lot of conversation surrounding conflict, communication styles, and boundaries. What we have yet to discuss, is what creates conflict.

What are the things that ruin good discussions and lead to a breakdown in communication?

This is where knowing your triggers and what can send you on a downward spiral to conflict come into play.

Learning what triggers you and the emotional reaction or response that comes along with it, can be the difference between a brief exchange and going to bed angry which we want to avoid as a much as possible.

Some examples of common triggers include:

I felt excluded.

I felt powerless.

I felt not listened to.

I felt scolded.

I felt judged.

I felt blamed.

I felt disrespected.

I felt no affection.

I felt unsafe.

I felt uncared for.

I felt lonely.

You weren't there for me when I was vulnerable and needed you.

I couldn't talk about my feelings without you going ballistic.

Once again, I was the bad guy, and you were innocent.

I was not being taken care of very well.

Your anger or yelling wasn't fair.

I had trouble with your sadness or despair.

I felt trapped.

I felt like you had no passion for me.

I couldn't ask you for what I needed.

I felt unloved.

I felt controlled.

I felt manipulated.

Triggers are typically left-over memories from a traumatic experience or experiences that created a huge detriment to your life.

The moments created during those experiences leave pockets of memories that when felt again, trigger past emotions and feelings that can't be forgotten or packaged away.

Whether it be the moment, you left home for good or the passing of a loved one who was very important to you, when communicating these experiences with your partner, be sure to explain the entire instance inclusive of emotions that can trigger a response for you.

This way, your partner is better equipped to handle these situations as they arise.

Conversely, being aware of triggers helps with proactively allowing yourself and your partner a better understanding of what to avoid, as certain phrases and keywords can subconsciously create an emotional trigger almost instantly.

This is because the language that we use can be altered dramatically due to the inflection in the voice and tone which can shift the climate of an argument or debate.

The following trigger words may not be as loud or harsh as curse words or calling names, but for as cliché as it may sound, words are powerful, and certain phrases serve as a very open channel to spreading blame and defensiveness.

"Can we talk?" or "We need to talk." I have never been able to figure out how those three words became such a trigger in a relationship.

They seem to manifest from nowhere and smack you clear in the face. These words can mean nothing, or they can mean everything to a relationship, but when they are uttered, the initial reaction is usually a negative one.

Work to remove these words from your list of emotional triggers by allowing your significant other the opportunity to say what they are thinking versus instantly becoming defensive.

Defensive cues show up as nonverbal gestures such as folding arms, sucking teeth, and deep sighs. These cues are highly noticeable, instantly creating conflict and tension where there was none.

"I'm sorry if/but…" Saying, "I'm sorry," by itself is a complete sentence. Adding the words 'if' or 'but' tend to negate the apology, again creating conflict and tension. The person you are apologizing to doesn't believe you due to the deflection in your statement.

If your apology is sincere, there should be no other action words required. Apologizing means you are accepting responsibility for your actions and wanting to make things right.

Using 'if' and 'but' create an open-ended conversation with room for finger pointing that turns your seemingly real apology into something negative.

A sincere apology should be simple and to the point, "I apologize for…" and let that be the end of it.

"What's wrong with you?" The word 'you' can be an upper or a downer depending on the context it's used in. The way the word 'you' is received also has a lot to do with tone and whether it's being used as a label or not.

As a label, 'you' can come across as judgmental and communicates blame in a way that will place the other party on the defensive, and of course, once you have put someone on the defensive, you must work harder to defuse the situation that could have otherwise been avoided.

When we use the word 'you' out of anger, frustration, or negativity, it becomes one of the most harmful words that we could use in that situation.

This is because it is blaming and shaming, as in the case of, "You never listen," or "You are thoughtless."

Although these statements may be true, it is better in this situation to refer to 'I' statements, so you are better able to communicate your thoughts and feelings without attacking the other person.

"Why are you so upset?" Remember the passive-aggressive communication style we discussed in chapter two? This is a perfect example of that communication style at work. Asking "why are you so upset?" is a deliberate and masked way of expressing covert feelings of anger.

As we discussed earlier, a passive-aggressive individual is a master at maintaining calm and acting shocked when individuals who are tired of their shenanigans, react out of anger or frustration.

Passive aggression will most assuredly lead to an escalation of negative emotions from other individuals involved and create more damage in the long-run.

People who actively participate in passive aggression create doubt surrounding their actions as an escape mechanism versus being able to accept responsibility for the hurt that they cause.

"It's Fine." Uh oh, if you're having a conversation with your significant other or anyone for that matter and mid-argument/disagreement they hit you with, "It's fine," duck for cover.

Frustration with those two words comes from the nonverbal cues that are being sent by a person who is bothered, yet either doesn't want to share their feelings or is not comfortable discussing them.

Although this can be misconstrued as being passive aggressive, it is the sign of a person not comfortable with making decisions or asserting their authority over the situation which can be draining to the other person.

It also becomes a disappointment for you because you are now forced to endure/enjoy choices that are made for you by others, quite possibly something you didn't want to do.

This statement is also used as a defense mechanism when the conversation becomes too uncomfortable to finish.

Not deciding or asserting yourself is not only energy-draining, but it also creates more distance between yourself and your partner.

We see so many skits and jokes surrounding the inability of someone not being able to answer seemingly simple questions like, "What do you want to eat?" "Where should we go?" or "What do you want to do today?"

Not being able to communicate your thoughts or feelings effectively may over time create resentment from your mate. This resentment comes from a place of feeling like decisions are solely their responsibility and that instead of a partnership or team relationship, they are alone in the decision-making process.

Being in a dedicated relationship takes work and a commitment, not only to the other person but yourself as well.

If you don't have a complete understanding of your needs, you will always have a hard time communicating with others and being in touch with what is troubling you.

Instead of using language that can be deemed passive or passive aggressive to spare someone else's feelings or your own, take a moment to consider how not answering or being indecisive affects the other person.

Communicating that you need a moment to think about the question before you answer it may be faced with some resistance, but in the long run, it will create an avenue for building patterns and a better understanding of your communication style.

In workplace conflicts, different needs are often at the heart of office disputes.

When we recognize the legitimacy of conflicting requirements and become willing to resolve them in an environment of compassionate understanding, it creates a lane for creative problem solving, team building, and improved relationships.

Key components needed to rectify conflict effectively include the ability to remain calm and alert in stressful situations, maintaining control over your emotions, and as previously stated, being able to communicate your needs effectively without finger pointing or appearing threatening to others.

Always remember to be aware of the feelings of others and to respect each other's differences.

Hot-Button Topics

As a child, I was taught that hot-button topics were to be avoided in familiar places such as the beauty salon, post office, elevator, on a first date or any public place where the subject matter can be deemed offensive.

These hot button topics were race, religion, and sexual orientation.

I was taught that these subjects have no business being discussed within earshot of people the conversation was not intended for nor should people feel trapped listening to a conversation that is offensive to their lifestyle.

As we approach the end of 2018, and the beginning of a world full of greater diversity, openness, and equality for all, I want to help with these conversations by listing hot topic keywords and phrases to avoid lessening the chances of creating conflict.

Words that highlight unequal treatment:
- racist
- bigot
- race
- the "n" word

Words or phrases that suggest you aren't interested:

- Whatever
- I don't care
- That has nothing to do with
- I'm not interested in
- I don't want to hear about it

Phrases that blame or imply blame, or suggest ignorance:

- Why don't you listen?
- You don't know anything about
- Apparently, you haven't
- Absolute words, such as 'always' and 'never'

Phrases that express an opinion

- I don't like you
- You are rude
- You have no right to

Phrases that suggest helplessness

- There's nothing I can do
- There's nothing you can do

Phrases that have a threatening undertone

- If you don't be quiet, I will throw you out
- Insulting me won't make me help you

Phrases that challenge an individual

- Go ahead, try to get me fired.
- Prove it.

●●●

Five Steps to Conflict Resolution

Conflict in the workplace is a common occurrence as you are bringing together individuals from different backgrounds with different personalities, different cultures, and different outlooks on life.

Being able to deal with conflict effectively has been the basis of this book, so I want to leave you with a quick five-step process to resolve conflict without having to bookmark each page relevant to specific situations.

Learning to handle conflict properly is a skill necessary for all relationships to grow and to flourish.

Remember, this five-step process is a quick reference point for resolving a specific conflict but learning the skills will help forever.

Step 1: How did the conflict start? The more information you have regarding what started the conflict, the easier it will be to resolve it.

As previously mentioned, use questions and open dialogue to identify what happened.

Questions like, "When did you begin to feel hurt or angry?" "Did something happen before today that may have incited this incident?" "How did these feelings start, was there a trigger?"

As a manager or supervisor, you must give each person an opportunity to share their side and explain what happened in their own words.

It will help you to understand what is going on and what may be keeping the conflict going. This also gives you an opportunity to remain neutral and impartial to both sides.

While your employees are speaking, it is encouraging to stay engaged and show active listening skills by offering an, "Ok," or "I see," so employees feel comfortable and are encouraged to continue to share information with you.

Step 2: Pay attention to the bigger picture. Most of the time, it isn't an individual incident that is inciting negative feelings, but the way the situation is being perceived by those involved.

Residual feelings from past experiences cause anger to fester and ultimately lead to disagreements or other visible signs of conflict.

The source of conflict might be a minor disagreement that happened months before, but the level of stress or frustration has grown to the point where the parties have begun attacking one another personally, instead of addressing the real point of contention.

Being in a neutral space, you can have them look beyond the incident that triggered the emotional response to see the real cause of the friction.

Once again, using probing questions always helps, like, "What do you think started this?" or "When do you think the problem first started?"

Step 3: Request solutions. After hearing both sides, the next step is to have each person identify ways to fix the situation and provide suggestions on what can be changed or done differently.

Again, question the parties to solicit their ideas: "How can you make things better?" As a manager or lead, you must be an active listener who pays attention to verbal tones and is a great reader of body language.

Your job is to get your employees to stop fighting and to start working together.

That means being able to steer the conversation away from finger-pointing toward resolving the conflict.

Step 4: Find a solution(s) that works for all parties. As a leader, you are working to find the most acceptable course of action to resolve the conflict.

Highlight positive points submitted by both parties not just from each other's perspective, but also from the perspective of benefits to the organization.

For instance, you may point out the need for more cooperation and collaboration to effectively address team issues and problems within the department.

Step 5: Agreement. We've reached the finish line! As the leader, you have the responsibility of getting the parties to agree with one or more of the solutions found in Step 4.

Some leaders will add a written warning to an employee's file that outlines solutions and timeframes that were agreed upon.

However, it may be enough to meet with the individuals to cover action plans for any possible future occurrences.

Self-Awareness

At the core of effective communication and conflict resolution, is self-awareness. Being self-aware is one of the essential components of being successful in just about every area of your life.

How you respond to conflict and external noise is controlled by an internal mental process.

Being self-aware also helps to highlight destructive behaviors, thought patterns, and unhealthy habits.

Being aware of these things, aids to better decision-making and a more positive behavioral response.

As a reference point, I want to provide you with ten exercises you can use every day to help you on your journey of becoming more self-aware.

Add these exercises to your daily routine and watch how your life changes for the better.

1. Practice saying no to yourself.

This must be number one on your list because this exercise is so vital.

"No," is a complete sentence that doesn't require any additional follow-up or explanation.

The ability to say no to yourself, to put off short-term satisfaction for long-term gain, is an important life-skill. The same goes for being able to tell others no.

Practicing this exercise on yourself will help strengthen your ability to express no to others and mean it.

The more you practice saying no to small challenges, the better you will be able to resist significant temptations.

Temptations surround us daily, social media, junk food, gossiping, and YouTube to name a few. Commit to saying no to five different temptations each day.

2. Accept yourself flaws and all.

No one is perfect, no really, they aren't, including you. Being aware of your flaws, without accepting them, doesn't help you at all.

Being self-aware of our flaws helps us to be less critical of others and prevents the hypocritical behavior.

Make it a daily habit of acknowledging your mistakes instead of making excuses.

Take some mirror time each day to highlight what you deem to be a flaw within yourself and work on that.

Be a reminder to yourself that being perfect is not the answer; being yourself is.

3. Stop reacting out of instinct.

Without self-awareness, people tend to respond when provoked instantly.

Being Self-aware provides you with the ability to assess situations objectively and rationally, without acting on biases and stereotypes.

When presented with a stressful situation or something someone says triggers an emotional response, stop for a moment, take a deep breath and evaluate the best way to respond.

4. How you speak to yourself is crucial.

Have you ever gone to do something and before you could follow through, you talked yourself out of it?

This is because there is non-stop commentary in our heads that is not always helpful. Debating back and forth with yourself over decisions can lead to stress, frustration, and depression.

Pay attention to how you respond to your successes and failures.

Do you chop your achievements up to luck or perfect timing and torment yourself after failures?

Break the cycle of negative self-talk by celebrating your wins and forgiving your losses.

Being tough on yourself needs to be balanced with self-compassion.

5. Watch your body language.

Are you proud of your poker face or does everyone know you don't have one?

Becoming aware of your body language and what it says not only helps the way you communicate with others, it also helps to boost your self-esteem.

Being aware of your body language; your posture and mannerisms also help to improve self-confidence.

Slouching, or taking a low-power-pose increases cortisol and feeds low self-esteem, while standing tall or taking a high-power-pose stimulates testosterone and improves your performance.

Using hand gestures helps with articulating your thoughts and affects how people respond to you.

Record yourself during a presentation so you can see yourself the way others see you allowing you to evaluate your posture and hand gestures.

Take the time also to watch videos of professional speakers mimicking their mannerisms that can help you improve your own.

6. Practice self-evaluation and reflection.

Write it down. For as cliché, as it may sound and regardless of how old we get, having a journal or a diary, helps us to keep track of our progress and keeps us on the path to greatness.

Use your writings to reflect daily about your progress surrounding stopping bad habits, reacting without thinking, making bad decisions and negative self-talk.

Set daily goals for yourself, use small breakthroughs as a stepping stone to broader goals.

At the end of each day, ask yourself questions that help guide you to a positive outcome.

Questions like, "What did I do well today?" and, "How can I improve on this tomorrow?" are great outlines for self-evaluation and reflection.

7. Meditate.

Meditation is a great way to relax, clear your mind and improve self-awareness.

Meditation teaches us how to transform our minds from harmful to positive, from disturbed to peaceful and from unhappy to happy.

By focusing entirely on your breathing, you're able to become aware of how your mind wanders, what thoughts distract you and how to snap out of it and bring yourself back to center.

When first beginning to meditate, try it for about ten minutes so as not to lose sight of why you are meditating in the first place.

Find a quiet place to sit, breathe in through your nose and out through your mouth.

Silently count your breaths reminding yourself to focus back in when your mind begins to wander.

8. Ask for constructive feedback.

From the inside looking out, it may seem as if we're doing it right and there aren't things we need to change. From the outside looking in, others may see things in you that you don't see in yourself.

Being open to and asking for regular constructive feedback cuts through any selfish or one-dimensional views you might have of yourself.

Constructive feedback must come from individuals whom you have mutual respect for, who understand you and will tell you what you need to hear, not what you want to hear.

9. Play Devil's Advocate.

Seeing things from a different point of view and a different perspective forces you to question your assumptions regarding a subject.

The way you choose to look at the world and react in certain situations, may not always be reasonable, so playing devil's advocate helps with changing or adjusting your thought process.

It becomes good practice to have an internal dialogue to see how your views hold up.

10. Work on your emotional vocabulary.

Has anyone ever told you that you need to be more in touch with your sensitive or emotional side? If so, it may be due to your lack of emotional response to a given situation.

Emotions create powerful physical and behavioral reactions that extend beyond happy or sad.

Being able to put your feelings into words creates influences your brain that can be therapeutic; however, if you aren't able to articulate how you feel, the frustration can be stress inducing.

Below is a list of feeling words that should be able to help identify and put a name on your emotions. Use this list to commit to increasing your emotional vocabulary with one new word each day.

OPEN	HAPPY	ALIVE	GOOD
understanding	great	playful	calm
confident	gay	courageous	peaceful
reliable	joyous	energetic	at ease
easy	lucky	liberated	comfortable
amazed	fortunate	optimistic	pleased
free	delighted	provocative	encouraged
sympathetic	overjoyed	impulsive	clever
interested	gleeful	free	surprised
satisfied	thankful	frisky	content
receptive	important	animated	quiet
accepting	festive	spirited	certain
kind	ecstatic	thrilled	relaxed
	satisfied	wonderful	serene

•••

By now, you should see that effectively dealing with and resolving conflict has a lot to do with proper communication and being able to communicate your thoughts and feelings effectively.

•••

CHAPTER FIVE

The Middle

We've reached the middle. How are you feeling? Do you feel empowered? Are you comfortable with the information that was shared?

The purpose of this book is to help you learn to communicate WITH your significant other, your child/children, your coworkers and subordinates versus talking AT them.

The last few chapters in this book are here as a guideline and a quick reference for boundaries, keywords, triggers, and tools that can help you on your quest to understanding, dealing with and resolving the conflict.

All the information we've discussed is made available in this recap of chapters one-four.

First up, we have some boundaries to avoid while in a conflict that can push your conversations or interactions downhill quickly.

Use this list as what NOT to do when communicating.

1. Using "You" Language –

Do you work in a specialized industry or around a group of people for most of your day? If so, your language to the rest of us may come off as strange or standoffish.

Take a moment to think about your audience before you begin to engage, and people won't feel like they must figure out what you are talking about or that you feel above them.

2. We didn't ask you that. – Stop answering questions that weren't asked of you. Also, stop giving out unsolicited advice.

Sometimes, people need to vent; be the ear and not the person trying to dominate the conversation.

3. Pay attention. – You know people can tell when you are listening to respond, correct?

Don't be the person waiting for the pause in the conversation, so that you can jump right in and start speaking.

People can also see when you're paying more attention to your cell phone and to everything else that's going on around them.

Be engaged, make eye contact and use gestures or keywords to acknowledge you're paying attention.

4. Focus. – When communicating with someone, it doesn't take much to miss the point especially if you aren't fully engaged as previously mentioned.

Missing the point of the conversation comes when you say things like, "I know but..." or "What about...?" Stay focused, so you don't become more of a hindrance than a help.

5. No judging or finger-pointing. – When a conversation is happening, it creates a huge barrier if you become judgmental, calls names, or criticize the speaker.

Allow the discussion to happen organically, ask questions to find out more information without making the situation hostile.

Conflict Resolution Skills

And now for the good stuff, the tips, and skills that will help to keep the tone of conversation on an even playing field.

I keep repeating it, but remember, effective communication doesn't happen overnight.

Perfecting your communication style takes practice and commitment to become someone indeed versed in the art of conversation.

Below are some skills opposite of the previously mentioned boundaries that will help develop your communication skills and communication style.

1. Active Listening – some ways to show that you are actively listening include: listening twice as much as you speak, listening with your whole body, being alert and genuinely engaged and interested in the other person, refraining from interrupting and using keywords to reflect on what was said and what you heard.

2. Non-Verbal Communication – remember the signals and gestures that were mentioned in chapter two, we must make mention of this style of communication because often, we communicate not only with words, but also with gestures and body language.

This means that active listening also involves recognizing and understanding non-verbal communication. A lot of times, we are unaware of the messages we are sending non-verbally.

Examples of non-verbal cues include eye contact (or lack thereof), facial expressions, silence, and hand, arm, and leg postures.

3. Ask Questions – when you are engaged in conversation with someone, asking questions shows you are listening and interested in what they are saying.

When thinking about the types of questions to ask, there are open-ended questions that begin with What and How or closed questions that start with Did, Do, Would, Will, Should, Could, Have, Must and Is.

More specific questions would begin with When, Where, Who, Which, How much, How many and How often.

Finally, there are thought-provoking questions like "Where do you see yourself?" or "What are your goals?"

4. Be Clear and Succinct – effectively communicating your thoughts and feelings means being clear and succinct when you speak.

This means that your words must be clear, articulate, and concise. Remember, sometimes less is more when it comes to communicating your thoughts and feelings.

5. Clarifying and Summarizing – as mentioned above, it is essential to make sure that you are actively listening and engaged in the conversation being held.

To ensure you heard the conversation correctly, reflect on what was said so you can clarify what you heard and effectively summarize what you heard from the other person.

This shows that you are listening, it also verifies you received the message correctly that they were trying to communicate.

6. Being Empathetic – having empathy for another person is the ability to understand and share the feelings of another.

Non-verbal cues are also present when actively listening and showing compassion for another person. This could be by way of a sad face or by dropping your shoulders.

Being empathic shows a person that it is ok to share their thoughts and feelings without judgment.

7. Providing Feedback – feedback is important! Being able to understand how your actions affect others is the key to growth and effective communication.

Whether you are receiving or giving feedback, the process can be a vulnerable, yet enlightening position to be in.

Find specific guidelines for providing feedback without judgment or finger pointing that can be used continuously across the fields of giving and receiving, so the process is fair and equal.

8. Developing Trust and Rapport – what does trust mean to you? How do you go about building trust with friends, family, and colleagues?

Is it something that happens naturally for you over time or does it require proof from the other party? Does it need building relationships based on honesty and integrity or do you look at actions over words? What about in relationships, how do you build trust there?

Being able to develop confidence and build a rapport with others, takes a lot of internal/behind the scenes work on ourselves before it can be given away.

Investing in someone and building a rapport is something that should be the goal. Sometimes, that comes with several bumps and bruises along the way.

9. Being Present – are you sick of reading this one yet? I know I've typed it three different ways from Sunday (old school saying), but this is because being present is a core component to most of the skills required to communicate effectively.

Being present means that you are actively listening, you are engaged, you recognize non-verbal cues, you're asking questions, and providing feedback.

Being present is a culmination of these skills that help reach an amicable resolution when it comes to conflict, as well as providing the other party with the comfort of knowing that you were present and available in the moment.

●●●

Using What You've Learned

Now that you've been given some tools to help you recognize and resolve conflict let's do a few exercises to see how you would use your new skills on everyday situations.

SITUATION #1
You're at your workstation, and you hear shouting coming from two coworkers. Each employee is raising their voice, calling names, and cursing to have their feelings heard to get their point across.

You see other employees in the area are beginning to look to you for answers while others are looking away and not wanting to become involved. What do you do? Do you intervene or not?

RESPONSE
Because the conversation is getting heated and has gone from a professional to a personal discussion, I recommend that you intervene.

You want to make sure that the individuals stay focused on professional matters while keeping personal issues entirely out of the conversation.

You may also consider having one-on-one meetings with each of them, but intervention would be the course of action to take so that both individuals have an opportunity to be heard.

SITUATION #2
At work, you notice one of your employees complains that they are the one who does everything in the office, mainly they are the one seeing projects through from beginning to end.

The complaints are creating tension in the office, so you decide to have a conversation with your employee to understand their frustration better.

To do this, you schedule a meeting with the employee to get to the bottom of this behavior and understand what is creating the conflict. What skill/skills should be used during this meeting?

RESPONSE
The skills you need to use in this situation are active listening skills. The reason for the meeting is to gain insight and to address their issues, not to highlight your position.

It's active listening skills that will allow you to get to the bottom of the situation and will also offer your employee the opportunity to share their concerns and know that their frustration has not gone unnoticed.

SITUATION #3
You're in a planning meeting at work when one of your team members presents a fantastic new idea. Before your team member could get their thought out thoroughly, another team member screams, "OMG, that was my idea! I can't believe you're going to share my idea as if it were yours!" and the two begin to argue back and forth.

The situation is getting out of control, and other team members look worried. As the team leader, what are your next steps?

RESPONSE
As a leader, it is essential always to remain neutral while acknowledging both sides.

Although the most critical issue is the idea, you can't have team members at odds on a project.

You must recognize both individuals, understand their points of view, and let them both know that the situation will be addressed in greater detail after the planning meeting.

During the follow-up meeting, you should work to have an understanding as to why one feels it's their idea versus the other, so you can successfully conclude and resolve the issue.

●●●

We've reached the end. How are you feeling? Did you learn something new? They say we're supposed to learn something new every day so I hope that *Creating a Middle* was able to help you with that.

I know a lot of the information is repetitive, but that is because most of the tools needed to communicate effectively, overlap one another.

A huge deciding factor in writing this book was the importance of having effective conflict resolution skills and how those skills open a lane for beneficial change to happen.

When issues and disagreements are continually ignored rather than being handled constructively, one of two things will happen; things will stay the same, or they will get worse.

However, when individuals can discuss their differences and work through them together, the stage is set for positive change to occur.

Although it might be more comfortable in the short term to leave things as they are (the band-aid), this struggle helps everyone involved in the conflict to work through these issues while developing stronger more lasting relationships.

Thank you so much for reading:

Creating a Middle: Conflict Tips for the Modern World.

References:

American Psychological Association. (2009). APA concise dictionary of psychology. Washington, DC: American Psychological Association.

I-Statements. (n.d.). Retrieved from http://www.austincc.edu/colangelo/1318/istatements.htm

Winters, K. (2003). Family Therapy. In Treatment of adolescents with substance use disorders. Rockville, MD: Substance Abuse and Mental Health Services Administration.

Gordon, Thomas. Origins of the Gordon Model. Gordon Training International. Retrieved on: 2012-01-17.

"I" Statements not "You" Statements, International Online Training Program on Intractable Conflict, Conflict Research Consortium, University of Colorado, USA

Social norms references

1. Marshall, G. Oxford Dictionary of Sociology
2. Jackson, J. (1965). "Structural characteristics of norms". In I.D. Steiner &

M. Fishbein (Eds.), Current studies in social psychology (pp. 301-309).
3. Lapinski, M. K.; Rimal, R. N. (2005). "An explication of social norms". Communication Theory. 15 (2): 127–147. doi:10.1093/ct/15.2.127.
4. Sherif, M. (1936). The psychology of social norms. NewYork: Harper.
5. ^ Cialdini, R. D. (2003). "Crafting normative messages to protect the environment" (PDF). Current Directions in Psychological Science. 12 (4): 105–109. doi:10.1111/1467-8721.01242.
6. https://en.wikipedia.org/wiki/Social_norm

Communication Toolkit - mensline.org.au
https://www.mensline.org.au/wp-content/uploads/2017/10/MLA-Communication-Toolkit-Communication-Patterns.pdf

https://gradebuddy.com/doc/2857516/i-messages-worksheet-role-plays

Responding to Conflict:
https://www.coursera.org/lecture/conflict-resolution-skills/active-listening-skills-lesson-2-NN70P

https://www.breakthecycle.org/blog/setting-boundaries-relationship

http://blog.mediate2go.com/2014/12/feeling-uncomfortable-set-boundary.html

Nonverbal Communication: Improving Your Nonverbal Skills ...
https://www.helpguide.org/articles/relationships-communication/nonverbal-communication.htm

9 Early Warning Signs of Workplace Conflict — Workplace ...
https://www.resologics.com/resologics-blog/2016/1/8/9-early-warning-signs-of-workplace-conflict

Ten Keys to Handling Unreasonable & Difficult People ...
https://www.psychologytoday.com/us/blog/communication-success/201309/ten-keys-handling-unreasonable-difficult-people

www.ingramcontent.com/pod-product-compliance
Lightning Source LLC
Chambersburg PA
CBHW070459100426
42743CB00010B/1692